The House Hustle

Within this book are key pieces of information that you need to ensure that you will be able to purchase a home as an entrepreneur. This information is tested, true, and verified by an insider in the industry with years of experience helping black entrepreneurs buy homes.

The Insider Secrets:

1. The ability to qualify for a mortgage is based on 3 things: your income, your assets, and your credit.

2. You make your money when you buy the house, not when you sell.

3. If you are a small business owner, you need to be in business for at least 2 consecutive years, and your income is averaged over the last 2 years to qualify for a mortgage. So, you need to have 2 years of positive income shown on your tax returns. The average of the two years worth of net profit on your tax return is what the bank thinks you make.

4. Your credit score should be at least a 620 if you want to get a mortgage in today's lending environment. Though you can possibly get a mortgage with a lower score, 620 is the ideal minimum standard.

5. You can get the seller to pay your closing costs using a seller's concession.

6. Your credit score and amount of down payment affect your rate. The lower the credit, the higher the interest rate. The lower the down payment, the higher the interest rate.

7. Do not co-sign on a loan for anyone if you can help it because his or her debt becomes yours. However with some lenders, car loans and mortgage liabilities can be waived if they are paid on time for 12 consecutive months, with no late payments by the person for whom you co-signed.

8. You do not need to put 20% down. You can do a down payment of as low as 3.5%, but you must have money for your closing costs in addition to your down payment. If you are a veteran, you can do 100% financing, but you still need to have the money for closing costs. Also, try to have some money for reserves. You can get gifts for your down payment from family in most cases. If you are putting less than 20% down, 5% must be your own funds on a conventional loan. On an FHA loan, all of your funds can be from gifts.

9. It's easier to get a mortgage when you still have a full-time job..

10. Owning a home and paying interest on a mortgage can save you money on your income taxes because of the mortgage interest tax deduction. Be sure to talk to your accountant about this.

Do you feel like you're just throwing money out the window every time you write that check to your landlord?

Had enough of renting?

Are you ready to finally own your p(a)lace?

Do you feel like you're being robbed when you see that rent check come out of your account?

Wouldn't it be nice if your landlord could finally fix that damn leaking sink? What if you were the landlord?

When you are your own landlord, you feel much more secure.

Introduction

You never know how strong you are until being strong is your only choice.

- Bob Marley

Home ownership is the cornerstone to financial wealth.

- Alfred Edmond, Jr., Chief Content Officer and former Editor-in-Chief, Black Enterprise Magazine

I heard Alfred Edmond say this in my last year of college when he spoke to a student group I co-founded. It was one of the best things I learned in college. I had no idea how much buying a home would improve my life when I bought my first apartment. Just from a peace of mind standpoint, it's huge. But from a financial standpoint, it is incomparable. When you write that check to the mortgage company, it's infinitely less painful than writing that check to your landlord. When you write that rent check to your landlord, you may feel like you're throwing your money away because you know that your rent is paying their mortgage and paying for their lifestyle. When you pay a mortgage, it's not completely painless, but you do get some peace of mind knowing that every time you cut that check, you are improving *your* financial condition. I have owned real estate for over 8 years and currently own 2 properties. As a result, my wife and I have options that simply would not be possible if we had not gone down this path. I know both from personal and professional experience that owning a home is one of the best gifts you can give yourself and your family.

You may have asked yourself, "what are the main benefits of buying a house?" In case you are on the fence about whether this is path is right for you, this is just a brief list I put together based on my own personal experience:

1. Peace of mind

2. Financial well-being

3. A place to call home that is your own

4. Freedom to customize your home any way you want

5. Satisfaction of knowing that you did it

6. Strengthens bonds with your family

7. Stable housing payment

8. A place to host friends and extended family when they are in need

9. A place to escape from family when you're in-need

10. Lasting positive effects on your children

Going from renting to owning is one of the most rewarding things you can do for yourself and your family. We know that in our hearts, of course, but what are the actual facts?

Well, for starters, it has a dramatic impact on your family, particularly your children. A Harvard study recently published in the Real Estate Economics Journal showed that children of homeowners performed 9% better in math and 7% higher in reading:

> We find that these results hold even after controlling for a large number of economic, social, and demographic variables. Owning a home compared with renting leads to 13 to 23% higher quality home environment, ceteris paribus (all other things being equal). The independent impact of homeownership, combined with its positive impact on the home environment, results in the children of owners achieving math scores up to nine percent higher, reading scores up to seven percent higher, and reductions in children's behavior problems of up to three percent.
> (http://www.jchs.harvard.edu/sites/jchs.harvard.edu/files/liho01-14.pdf)

While many renters attempt to provide the same stability for their children, some factors may be out of their control because they live in properties that aren't their own. A study, recently published in the Journal of Urban Economics, found that:

> When households included a 17-year-old, a 1% rise in prices that year resulted in about 0.9% higher annual income for the child later in life—if the parents owned the home. If the parents were renters, however, it was a different story. Indeed, if the parents of the 17-year-old rented their home, a 1% rise in the home's price resulted in 1.5% lower annual income for the child. (http://www.wsj.com/articles/study-salary-advantage-goes-to-children-of-homeowners-1428894132)

Secondly, owning a home has a long-term effect on your net worth. Homeownership is the cornerstone to wealth. The latest Census Bureau data on wealth indicated that the median American household had a net worth of $68,828 in 2011 (half of households had more and half had less). Of the 78 million families that owned their own home, the median net worth was $161,826, while the median net worth for the 37 million families who rent was $2,066. If you take out the value of their home equity, owners had a median net worth of $47,297. (https://www.census.gov/people/wealth/)

Thirdly, studies show that homeowners have an overall greater sense of well-being. A University of Massachusetts, Amherst study showed:

> Owners are higher than renters in self-satisfaction and are more likely to believe that they can do things as well as anyone else, are more sure that their lives will work out the way that they want, score lower on a scale of depression, show higher happiness with life in general, and rate themselves higher in physical health.
> (http://content.knowledgeplex.org/kp2/img/cache/documents/1374.pdf)

These are facts discovered by people who spend their entire lives trying to figure these things out. It is pretty self-evident that owning a home will help you in life.

Now, I know that many people may be turned off because of the recent housing crisis. But these things happen in any market. The stock market crashes every so often, and then recovers. Similarly, the job market crashes and then recovers. The technology industry has a bubble, crashes, and then recovers. Ebb and flow is true of all markets, housing included. We are in the midst of a housing recovery right now. Bloomberg News reports show that housing is in full swing at the moment. (http://www.bloomberg.com/news/articles/2015-07-22/housing-recovery-in-full-swing-as-u-s-sales-at-eight-year-high)

But why is home ownership the cornerstone to financial wealth? Well, for two reasons:

1. **Leverage**: Leverage is being able to do a lot with a little.

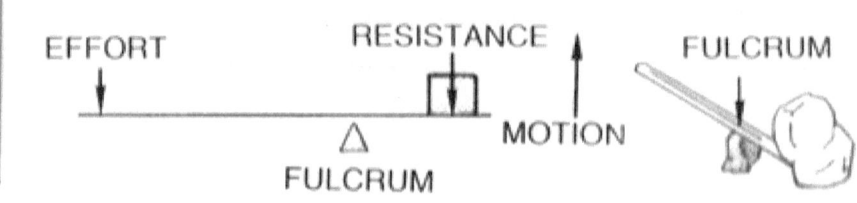

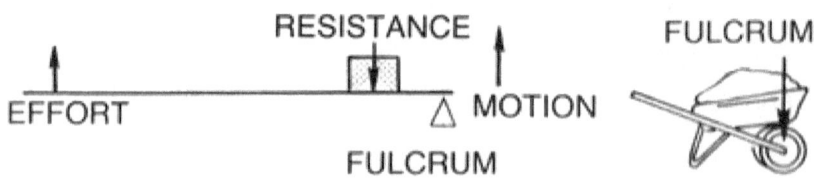

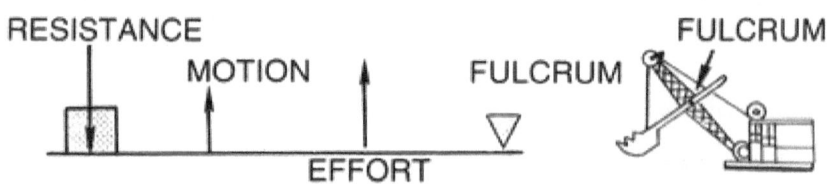

(https://en.wikipedia.org/wiki/Lever)

If I told you that you could invest $1000 in something and make a $10,000 profit, you would ask if I used to work for Bernie Madoff, right? But what if there was such an investment that was actually legit? What many people overlook is that this scenario is possible when you invest using leverage. Leverage is controlling a large asset with a significantly smaller amount of money. When you buy a home, you are using leverage. You're getting control of a huge asset, which is the house, with a relatively small investment, which are the down payment and closing costs. The mortgage provides the leverage by making up the difference between the price of the house and the money you have to put down. Without this leverage, you would have to come up with all of the cash to buy the home.

When you use a mortgage to buy a house, you are using the power of leverage to own something of great value by investing a significantly smaller amount. Let's say you buy a house for $250,000 and you made a 10% down payment. You would pay out of pocket roughly $29-38,000 when you add in closing costs and other fees. But in the end you would have an asset worth $250,000. When that house is worth $255,000, you just made a $5,000 profit on a $38,000 investment (if you paid the most in closing costs). That's roughly a 13% return. What are you currently earning in interest on your savings account? Exactly. There aren't many investments out there paying that much that aren't risky as hell. And even if you do find one that makes sense, it won't provide you with shelter, peace of mind, and a tax deduction. Put another way, if you wanted to buy $250,000 worth of stock, how much money would you need to come up with? $250,000 if you bought without using margin. But when you use leverage, you still get the profits but put up a fraction of the cash and get all of the gains.

2. Inflation:

Do you remember when you were younger and a Snickers bar was about 50 cents? If you haven't been to the corner store recently, it's now a dollar or more. That is inflation. According to inflationdata.com, average inflation in the US has been 3.22% for roughly the past 100 years. That means if you're around my age range--anywhere from end of GenX to mid-millennial--we will see prices double at least twice in our lifetimes.

(http://inflationdata.com/Inflation/Inflation_Rate/Long_Term_Inflation.asp). And if you're older than the millennial generation, you know firsthand what inflation is. If you bought a house in 1982 for $250,000, using the rate of inflation that the US has experienced during that time, theoretically, it would be worth $613,305.70. Of course, this wouldn't be the case for everyone because every area appreciates at a different rate. But look at this example: If you bought a house for $250,000 in 1932, according to US inflation statistics, it would be worth $4,320,000. You can check it out yourself at usinflationcalculator.com. Think about that. $2,000 today will be roughly $15,853.50 when we are in old age. Luckily for us, home values increase with inflation as well. You're going to be a homeowner soon so you'll be able to capture some of these gains. Ask any older person you know who has paid off their house how much they originally bought it for. My grandparents bought their home for $35,000 in 1963. Today, it is worth about $525,000, which is more than ten times its original value. That could be you in 50 years. Long term, owning a home gives you one of the best ways to benefit from inflation.

Me

I graduated from Rutgers University (go Scarlet Knights!) and have been working as a mortgage banker for Fortune 500 banks and financial institutions for over 10 years. I frequently consult with entrepreneurs who are completely clueless on how to qualify to buy a home. This problem is particularly pronounced with my clients who are Black and Brown. Many are so busy running their businesses that they don't get a chance to really research what goes into orchestrating a home purchase. I once had a client in the art business who was wildly successful in his business of art dealing, had a ton of assets, was doing a massive amount of sales, and had great credit. He wanted to buy an apartment in a swanky part of Brooklyn and was really excited and eager to reap the benefits of his success. I was eager to help him do so as well. We spoke many times while I was helping him get prepared to buy. When I finally got a copy of his tax returns in my hands, the amount of business expenses he had claimed on his tax return was so high that he wasn't profitable enough to qualify. It was a major disappointment for both him and me.

I bought my first apartment for $85,000 in Brooklyn NY in 2007 (I know I found a crazy steal of a deal). I put 10% down, which was $8,500. Then, I paid about $7,000 in closing costs, which seems like a lot, right? I know. It's almost as much as the down payment. I bought during the Wild Wild West days of real estate when there were a fewer protections for homebuyers. Today, you are a lot safer. Anyway, about a year later the property was worth about $100,000. My wife and I did a lot of work on it and improved it over time. After 5 years, it was already worth $200,000. At the time of this writing, it is worth about $460,000. At the end of the day, I spent $13,500 and by year one, I made $15,000 in profit. This rate of appreciation is not typical in every market, but in fast growing areas, you can be sure that you will see appreciation that will benefit your bottom line, but more on that later. This is what you're going to do by taking advantage of leverage, inflation, and price appreciation once you buy your place. I've done countless loans for people who bought right and are reaping the benefits now. A client of mine, who we'll call Monique to protect her privacy, had a similar situation, which I want to share with you. When she bought her apartment for $425,000 in Brooklyn in 2011, she put 20% down, which was

$85,000. By 2013, it was worth $475,000. So, after spending $85,000, she made a profit of $50,000. Today it is worth about $600,000. Not bad, Monique.

Many business owners I speak to don't know where to start looking to figure out how to buy a home. In Black and Brown communities, this issue is even more apparent for a number of reasons. In this country, Blacks and other people of color have been locked out of the benefits of homeownership for generations. There are many, many causes of this but the two most important factors that still have lingering effects today are redlining (https://en.wikipedia.org/wiki/Redlining) and restrictive housing covenants (http://www.bostonfairhousing.org/timeline/1920s1948-Restrictive-Covenants.html). Our people have been locked out of homeownership and building equity for so long that I know many are disillusioned and frustrated. Just a few short years ago, it seemed like every bank was paying massive fines for predatory lending in the Black community. We are still suffering from these offenses. Being informed is the best way to avoid getting ripped off. From blockbusting to redlining, our parents and grandparents had it way harder than we have it today. Not to say that it's easy for us, it's just easier for us than it was for them.

When my grandparents were buying their home, there were government-sanctioned programs that locked them out of buying a home in the best areas even if they had the money (redlining, as mentioned above). In the early 2000's, Wells Fargo and other banks gave people of color mainly subprime loans, even if we had great credit, income, and a down payment. There have been numerous lawsuits filed and settlements paid out. Unfortunately, various forms of predatory lending are still happening today. Notwithstanding all that, we can still get homes and do what we want to do. With the recent changing of all the laws, there are a lot more protections for us. You can thank Obama and the Dodd Frank bill.

According to the 2013 Federal Reserve Home Mortgage Disclosure Act data, African Americans bought 5.7% of all homes in 2013 and have bought roughly 5% of all homes in the US for the past 10 years, while whites have bought about 70%. We also have a loan denial rate of about 25% in the past 10 years, while whites have a rate of 12%. We have the highest rate of denials for credit reasons at about 30%.

For the past 10 years, 44% of our applicants had scores between 550 and 650. Our second most common issue is debt-to-income ratio. (http://www.federalreserve.gov/pubs/bulletin/2014/pdf/2013_HMDA.pdf)

Though many roadblocks still exist, today we are far more fortunate than our forebears. These roadblocks can be overcome by having the right information in hand and being educated. That is the reason for this book.

For most people outside of the real estate industry, the ins and outs of getting a mortgage and buying a home might as well be the instructions for programming Google's algorithms. I wrote this book to help get Black small business owners over that hump. I have put together the top ten tips to buying a home but I have also included some key bonus tips that will give you some of the insider secrets to being a successful homeowner and the keys to building a legacy.

Most of these secrets are hidden in plain sight. Some of them are common sense and some of them are totally counterintuitive. I am writing this book to cut through all the confusion and frustration of trying to get a home. So without further ado, here are the tips in their entirety.

The Secrets (again):

1. The ability to qualify for a mortgage is based on 3 things: your income, your assets, and your credit.

2. You make your money when you buy the house, not when you sell.

3. If you are a small business owner, you need to be in business for at least 2 consecutive years, and your income is averaged over the last 2 years to qualify for a mortgage. So, you need to have 2 years of positive income shown on your tax returns. The average of the two years worth of net profit on your tax return is what the bank thinks you make.

4. Your credit score should be at least a 620 if you want to get a mortgage in today's lending environment. Though you can possibly get a mortgage with a lower score, 620 is the ideal minimum standard.

5. You can get the seller to pay your closing costs using a seller's concession.

6. Your credit score and amount of down payment affect your rate. The lower the credit, the higher the interest rate. The lower the down payment, the higher the interest rate.

7. Do not co-sign on a loan for anyone if you can help it because his or her debt becomes yours. However with some lenders, car loans and mortgage liabilities can be waived if they are paid on time for 12 consecutive months, with no late payments by the person for whom you co-signed.

8. You do not need to put 20% down. You can do a down payment of as low as 3.5%, but you must have money for your closing costs in addition to your down payment. If you are a veteran, you can do 100% financing, but you still need to have the money for closing costs. Also, try to have some money for reserves. You can get gifts for your down payment from family in most cases. If you are putting less than 20% down, 5% must be your own funds on a conventional loan. On an FHA loan, all of your funds can be from gifts.

9. It's easier to get a mortgage when you still have a full-time job..

10. Owning a home and paying interest on a mortgage can save you money on your income taxes because of the mortgage interest tax deduction. Be sure to talk to your accountant about this.

There two 2 components to purchasing a home and we are going to go through each one. Number one is The Mortgage. Number two is

The House. I will go through each one and all of the factors you need to think about comprehensively.

The Mortgage

Overview

Being able to get a mortgage to buy a house is based on 3 things about you:

1. Your credit

2. Your income

3. Your assets

Unless you're independently wealthy, you'll probably get a mortgage to buy your home. Getting the mortgage is really the crux of the whole thing. That's why I'm covering it first. Think of these factors as the three wheels of a tricycle. All three have to be working in tandem for the tricycle to work. Your income is how much net profit you make from your business(es). Your assets are how much money you have to put toward the down payment and closing costs, in addition to what you have left over. This includes your savings, stocks, bonds, cash value in life insurance, the value of your 401k, your annuities, and any other accounts that you can readily convert to cash. Your credit is your credit score, the amount of debt you have and the monthly payments on those debts as shown on your credit report with the three credit bureaus Equifax, Experian, and TransUnion.

Mortgages come in terms of 15, 20, 25, or 30 years. The longer the term of your loan, the lower your monthly payment is. Keep that in mind when you are deciding which loan to apply for.

There are generally 2 types of mortgages: fixed and adjustable (aka ARM). Fixed means the rate stays the same for the entire term of the loan. So, if you have a 30-year fixed mortgage, your rate stays the same for the entire 30 years. Adjustable or ARM (adjustable rate mortgage) are loans where the rate remains fixed for a set amount of time -- typically 3, 5, 7, or 10 years. After this period, the rate adjusts to the market rate. In this case, the loan is still on a 30-year repayment schedule, but you just don't know what the rate will be in the future. If the market rate is higher, your mortgage payment will go up. If the market rate is lower, your payment will go down. There are merits to both types of loans but the safe bet is the 30-year fixed mortgage because you don't have to worry about the payment ever changing again. So let's now delve into each of the critical factors of you being able to get a mortgage.

Credit

Credit is sometimes more important than having cash. To purchase a home you absolutely must have your credit in order. You need to have at least decent credit to buy a home. What is decent credit? Well, lenders use the middle of your 3 credit scores. In addition, they use their own credit scoring models. It's like the Olympics; they throw out the highest score, throw out the lowest score and go with the middle. You may have a great score when you check your credit online, but it may not be good enough when the bank runs your credit. This is because of the credit scoring model that the lenders use specifically for mortgages. The closest you are going to get to seeing what the banks see is by using myfico.com. In my experience at the time of this writing, when compared with lenders' mortgage credit scoring models, they are the best. Better than Credit Karma. MyFico.com is usually + or - 5-10 points from the actual score lenders will reference. Ideally, you should keep track of your credit weekly, but no less than monthly. Set a reminder if you need to. For monthly tracking you can use creditkarma.com as well. It is free. If you have a Capital One credit card account, it comes with a credit tracker on the app and web. Use it. Keeping track of your credit lets you know what's happening as you make different moves credit-wise.

You must have at least 3 trade-lines for at least one year. A trade-line is an account that reports to the three credit bureaus, such as an American Express Card or Chase car loan.

No credit? Pay for everything in cash because you don't want to be in debt and pay interest? No problem. That's a great strategy for the long term once you have credit, but for now you will have to compromise to get your credit in a state where banks will lend to you and learn how to manage it. Here are some of the secrets on how you establish it:

Establishing Credit

1.   Open a store credit card from a store such as Target, The Gap/Old Navy, Children's Place, etc. and use it very lightly for one year. Maintain a balance on the card that does not exceed more than 30% of the credit limit. Pay on time every month, no matter what.

2.   Take out a fixed loan from your bank for something that you were going to purchase anyway. For example, if you were going to purchase furniture or a television, take out a loan to purchase it. Only do this if you already have the money to buy the item. You are only going to pay the loan payments for 3-6 months then pay off the entire balance. This will cause you to pay interest, but it will be a

worthwhile expense because this will help you establish your credit and save you a lot more in the long term.

3. Open a secured credit card and make a small purchase on it every month. Pay off the balance in full at the end of each month. You can use it for something like groceries or gas. A secured credit card is a credit card where you deposit a certain amount of money with the bank and they give you a credit line for the amount that you deposited. For many of them, you get your deposit back after a certain amount of time determined by the lender.

Credit Repair

Bad credit? Did you get caught up with credit cards in college and are still feeling the effects? No problem. Here are some secrets on how to deal with that (you can skip this section if you already have your credit in order):

1. Figure out what bad information is on your credit report. It could be a misspelled name, an incorrect address or workplace. But most importantly you want to look for any accounts that are not yours. Secondly, but just as important, you want to look for accounts that have been paid off but still show balances.

2. Dispute any inaccurate information on your credit report. This could include the above from number one, but also includes incorrect reporting of late payments, entire debts that have been paid off but still appear, collections stemming from a clerical error, etc. You will dispute this information on your credit report by writing to the credit bureaus. Do this in actual writing. Like pen and paper,

envelope and stamp. Write them an official letter detailing which information is incorrect. In the letter, you will also tell the credit bureaus what the information should be and you will provide any proof you have to that effect. You can dispute online, but putting it in writing is the best route. An actual person has to open the letter, record it, and prepare a response. Actual labor is required to resolve your dispute. This can only help your case.

3. Do not just immediately pay off anything that is currently in collections. Doing that could actually make your credit worse. You need to negotiate with them to get the best outcome for your credit.

Call each creditor, and I do mean call--not email or send a request through their website--and request to speak to an agent. Tell them you want to work out a payment plan to resolve the debt. Negotiate with them to pay less than what is owed and ask them to provide you a letter stating that once this is paid they will remove it from your credit. Start the negotiation at 25% of your balance. Try not to go above 50%. Do not accept any circumstance in which the creditor will report, "settled for less than amount owed" on your credit. That is like a black hole for your credit score. Please ask and get written confirmation from the collection agency that this will not be on your report before paying even a single dime. Many times, your debt has been written off as a loss from the original creditor and sold to a collection agent for pennies on the dollar. Anything they collect from you is pretty much profit. Once the debt is paid off, remind them to remove it from your credit. These little steps can be tedious, but they are worth it in the end. This is where that written confirmation is key. Once they start dragging their feet (and some definitely will), refer them to the letter. Also, keep all proof of payment for your records. There are always staff changes at these companies and they may claim they have no record of your case. Once again, you refer them to the letter and your receipts. Once these steps are done, you have to reestablish your credit. Follow steps from the previous section.

Credit Monitoring

In both cases you will want to continually monitor your credit to see the effects of your actions on cleaning up or establishing credit.

To monitor your credit, you can use Credit Karma, which is free and gives you an updated credit report once a week.

You can also use My Fico. This option is not free, but it gives you, in my opinion, the most accurate approximation of what your credit score is from a lender's perspective.

Basics of Managing Credit

One key to maintaining good credit is to keep your total amount of debt you've taken out at 30% of your total credit limit or below. Also, try not to max out any cards. The credit bureaus call a card that has 90% of the limit used maxed out. If you find that your credit balance is above that, request to increase your credit lines, get more credit, but most importantly manage your credit use. The second key is to always pay your bills on time…every time. On-time payments and amount of debt outstanding (debt to credit ratio) account for **60%** of your credit score. These together comprise the number one factor in your credit rating.

Another very important thing to know about credit is that you want to avoid co-signing for other people's loans for at least 2 years before buying home. This is super important. When you apply for a mortgage, the mortgage company is going to divide monthly debt payments by your income. That means that all your minimum monthly payments on your debts on your credit report like credit cards, student loans, car loans, furniture loans, car leases, AND loans you have co-signed for, like mortgages and car loans, will be counted. A lot of times, people need someone to co-sign a loan for them to qualify. If you are the co-signer, that debt gets counted as your liability until it is paid off. Some banks will let you discount debt such as a car loan or mortgage payment from your monthly debt if the person you co-signed for pays the account for 12-24 consecutive months on time out of their own account. They will also ask you to prove it by providing cancelled checks or bank statements. Not every bank does this but many do. So if you've already cosigned, it's too late to follow this, but you may be able to avoid having the debt counted against you if they are paying on time, for at least 12 months, from their own account.. This only works for loans -- not credit cards or lines of credit. If you have not co-signed as yet, take this into consideration before signing on that dotted line for someone.

So, what does your credit score need to be to get a loan? Ideally, your credit score should be at least 620 to qualify for a mortgage. A

620 score basically says you pay most of your bills most of the time OR you spend a little more than you earn. That is barely good enough for a mortgage. With a credit score, you want to at least prove that you don't spend more than you make. As you spend more than you earn, generally your credit goes down. This is because in order to spend more than you have, you must rely on credit. As you use more credit than you can pay back in a month, your outstanding debt increases. This increases your debt to credit ratio (which we talked about earlier) and this decreases your credit score. Once you even that out, you'll be in a better position. You can also have a 620 if you had bills that you didn't pay in the past and you never got around to fixing it on your credit report. These two examples cover most of the reasons why someone's credit is at this level. But the good news is that they are both easily fixed. Start first with first paying down some debt. You've got to budget paying it off every month. Cut your expenses, which is something everyone can do. Make a lifestyle change if you need to, but get that together in order to get your credit together.

Lastly, you need to be aware of credit inquiries. When you get your credit run by a lender or an institution that is going to lend you money for any reason, they "run your credit". This credit run is called a credit inquiry. That includes leases, car loans, credit cards, furniture loans, student loans, bank loans, business lines of credit, business credit cards, etc. When you apply for any of these, it hurts your credit. When you apply for credit, the credit bureaus see it as an increased risk of you defaulting. They figure that if you take on the new credit card or loan that you've applied for, you have increased your debt load making it more statistically probable that you will default in the future. They have studied this for years and know the numbers. They have a whole system as to how they work it out. Now, when you check your own credit it doesn't hurt you. You can run your own credit on creditkarma.com, myfico.com, freecreditreport.com or similar sites and there is no effect. These are just informational inquiries, so they don't cause any alarm with the credit bureaus. However, when a lender runs your credit it does hurt you. Credit inquiries stay on your credit report for at least 2 years. An initial credit inquiry can seriously affect your score in certain cases. Try to keep them to a minimum. There is one caveat to this when it comes to shopping for a mortgage, which I will expand on in the next section.

Establishing Business Credit

When it comes to credit, one very important benefit to being a business owner is that you can establish business credit. This allows you to have some of your major liabilities be the responsibility of your business. This means that the liabilities will not affect your debt to credit ratio. Do loans under your business if you can and get them off your credit because then they don't count towards your personal debt. When you have business credit, f you have a big loan that you need to take out for business purposes, you can take out the loan on your business credit rather than your personal credit.

Establishing business credit starts with opening a business bank account. Once your business is legally established, you can go to your local bank and open up an account. Once you do this, you will start to see offers come in the mail for business credit cards and loans. Take one of the offers. This will be your business' first tradeline and you can build from there as outlined in the steps above about personal credit.

Credit and Getting a Mortgage

With a 620 score you can get a loan. Some lenders will lend you money with as low as a 500 FICO score, but that can get dicey. At a 500 score, you'll have to put down no less than 10% and possibly pay a much higher interest rate. A solid 620 score will get you a conventional mortgage with most lenders..

Now while you can still get a conventional loan with a 620 score, the interest rate will be higher than it would be if you had a higher credit score. To get the absolute best pricing on a loan, you will need around a 740 FICO score. As your score goes up, your rate goes down. You should strive to always keep your credit score above 700. This way, no matter what life may throw at you, you can qualify for mortgage financing. Now I know this may not always be possible in all cases but it is something that you want to always keep in mind. If your credit score is below 700, don't feel bad about yourself. Contrary to popular belief, a bad credit score obviously doesn't mean you're a bad person or that you're irresponsible. This is simply not true. It just means that you had some things come up on your credit report that either haven't been dealt with yet or are in the process of being resolved. I know tons of people who have less-than-stellar credit for various reasons and they are excellent and responsible people.

In some cases, lenders will require that you have a credit score higher than 620 to be able to make a down payment of less than 20%. You can shop around and poll different banks to find out which ones will allow for a smaller down payment based on your credit score. There is a specific type of loan called an FHA loan that will allow you to make a down payment as low as 3.5% regardless of your score once you meet a certain minimum credit score. Be sure to research this option as well.

When it comes to mortgages, the caveat to credit inquiries negatively affecting your score is that when you are shopping around for a mortgage, you can get your credit run by multiple lenders in a certain period of time and it will only have the negative impact of one inquiry. This is because you are allowed to shop around. The credit bureaus recognize that it is prudent to shop around for a mortgage and that you are not reasonably going to get more than one mortgage at a time. You need to do all the shopping within a 1-2 week period though. Past that time period, the inquiry will hurt you. This goes back to the previous reason of the bank thinking that you are about to take out another loan, which will jeopardize your financial standing.

Income

You need to be in business for at least 2 consecutive years to get a loan as an entrepreneur and your net profit has to be positive when averaged over the past 2 years' tax returns. The bank says to itself, "Hey, this man/woman wants to borrow X dollars. How do I know he/she will pay me back? Does he/she even have a job? Where is the money going to come from?"

We all know that most businesses fail within the first year. Lenders know this, too. They figure that once you've made it past that 2 year hump, you've battled a few dragons and come out the hero. If you do not have 2 consecutive years of business operations (on your taxes), the lender will not let you count your business income. This is true even if it is your only income. There are some banks that will let you use only 1 year, but you really have to search for them. They are likely not the bank you're dealing with now. A very important thing to note is that when it comes to averaging your income over the past 2 years, if your income from last year is more than your income this year, the lender will actually use this year's figure as your income.

You should get an accountant if you are self-employed because he or she can help you get your paperwork in order before you need a loan.

The important thing here is that you have to file your taxes and pay them. In order for the mortgage company to know how much you make, they must be able to see it in writing. Now, I know this may sound elementary and common sense, but it is true. Lenders will look at your NET profits for the past 2 years and average them over the two years to arrive at what your current income is. Again, if your income is less this year than the year before, they will use the lower figure as your current income, even if the average is higher. This is because their thinking is that the business is declining, so you will not make more than you did the previous year. The bank's job is not to have faith in what you will do in the future--that's your job. Now I'm not commenting on whether the bank is right or wrong for thinking this way, but look at it this way; when you have a regular job, when do you start feeling sure that you won't get fired or leave? Usually after about a year, right? Usually by about the second year you know that you've got it down enough where you will be fine for the foreseeable future. Your business is your job and it's a similar thought process for the lender. This is important.

Debt To Income Ratio (DTI)

Lenders use your net profit income as the gauge of how much you can afford to pay back. The factor that they use is called the debt to income ratio (DTI). You don't need to remember that term, but you do need to understand the concept. The DTI is basically your monthly debt service versus your income. The bank adds up all the monthly debts that you pay and divides that number by your income. The monthly debts include everything on your credit report with a monthly payment. They take the minimum monthly payment due on the credit report for each account as part of the factor. They do not use the payment that you choose to make above the minimum amount due. Your debt to income ratio needs to be below 43-45% for conventional loans and 50% for FHA loans. You can calculate this by adding up all the minimum monthly payments on your credit report PLUS the payment for the new loan you are about to obtain and dividing that by your monthly income.

The Mortgage Payment

When you pay your mortgage, you are paying the loan payment in addition to: PMI (if you put down less than 20%), the property taxes, and the homeowner's insurance. All these items need to be included in the payment to arrive at an accurate DTI.

Entrepreneur Versus Employee

It's easier to get a loan as an employee, so if you're thinking about making the jump and you still have a job, buy a house first.

When you have a job for 2 years or more, the lender looks at you as less of risk because they figure that you having a job for 2 years is a good indicator of you continuing to have a job. Having a job is a steady source of income, which means you are likely to repay the loan. If you are an entrepreneur who has not yet transitioned to doing your business full-time, think long and hard before making the transition before buying a house. Once you transition to a full-time business owner, you have to show 2 consecutive years of profitability in your federal tax filings before being able to qualify for a mortgage.

Assets

The days of no down payment (100% financing) are over, unless you are a veteran. If you are a veteran, you have access to the VA loan. That allows you to purchase a home with 100% financing and no PMI. It's great. Note, however, that you will still need money for closing costs. In order to get in this home buying game, you must furnish at least some sort of money for a down payment and closing costs. If you only have money for the down payment, it is not enough. Closing costs are a major consideration that you must budget for. You can get a mortgage with as little as 3.5% down on an FHA mortgage as mentioned earlier. The down payment is a percentage of the purchase price. So for a $100,000 house, that is $3,500. In addition to this, you must have money for whatever the closing costs will be. It varies by location. For example, in New York City, if you are buying a single-family house, your closing costs could be in the 2.7% range of the loan amount. New York City is an area with some of the highest closing costs, so I use it as an example. It is usually less in other areas. There are a lot of details regarding closing costs that are beyond the scope of this book, but the point is you must have some money saved up to get this done. No money saved = no house. There are a number of programs that help you buy with down payment assistance and closing cost assistance. But they are only assistance. Do not plan to buy a house with no money. It will not work in most cases.

If you are not applying for an FHA mortgage, the minimum down payment you can make on a home with a conventional mortgage is 5%.

Now the main thing to note about putting a lower down payment (lower than 20%) is that first, your payment will be higher, and second, you will have to pay what's called PMI. This is private mortgage insurance. On an FHA mortgage it is call MIP, mortgage insurance premium. This is an insurance that protects the lender in case you default. It does not pay the mortgage on your behalf in case you pay late. I know it sounds crazy and not right, but unfortunately that's how it works. On the bright side, this PMI lets you buy the house using less than 20% down. I mean realistically, saving 20% of the purchase price can take you quite a long time. By the time you're able to do that, prices of homes may have gone up so much that you can only afford less house that you hoped for. How it works is, depending on your credit score and amount of down payment, you will have to pay a certain percentage of the loan amount in addition to your mortgage payment, taxes, and insurance. However, if you do put down 20% or more, you will not have to pay any PMI.

Compensating Factors

Sometimes, with all of these things we discussed--DTI, credit score, assets--one of them doesn't add up and you're outside of the scope of what a lender will deem acceptable. Looks like it's all over, right? Wrong. If you are weak in one area and strong in others, you can use what is called a compensating factor. This is where you are over and above in one area of qualifying. For example, you may not make enough money to qualify, but you have a large amount of money in the bank for reserves. This would be a compensating factor that the bank could use to possibly approve your file. Some of the main compensating factors are:

1. A large amount of liquid assets above the money needed for down payment and closing costs
2. High credit score
3. Length of employment at the same place
4. Living in the same place for a long time
5. Profession or industry
6. Co-signer
7. High income
8. High down payment
9. Loan to value ratio - this is the ratio of the amount that is owed on the loan over how much the property is worth. The lower this ratio is, the more equity you have in your property.

The House

Shop For A Home

Now that you know what it takes to get the money to buy a home, you can actually go shopping for a home. Here are some important guidelines for choosing a home to buy.

DO NOT PICK A HOME BECAUSE OF JUST 1 FACTOR. HAVE AT LEAST 3 FACTORS AS TO WHY YOU WANT THAT PARTICULAR HOUSE.

When times get tough with that house--which at some point they will--you will need to have a few extra reasons other than just price or location as to why you connect to owning it. Most houses have something wrong with them. It's unfortunate but true. At some point that one thing is going to make you crazy. You will wonder if you made the right decision. There has to be more than just price or location or only one factor that helps you justify the purchase. For example, factors such as knowing that it will be big enough for your growing family or an aging parent, schools, light exposure are examples of factors that can work in concert with price and location to help determine whether the house is the right fit for you.

DON'T <u>NOT</u> BUY A HOME JUST BECAUSE OF CURRENT COSMETIC ISSUES

The toilet is dirty, you don't like the wallpaper, the blinds are ugly; these things, although they matter, don't really matter that much. You are about to make a purchase that will likely put you in debt for for decades. Do not make the wrong move because the previous owner painted the living room orange. You're going to be living there for a while and will have the option to change everything cosmetic about that house. Some fixes are quite easy and fast. Cosmetic issues have stopped so many people from owning the house of their dreams. When buying a home, sometimes you have to have a little vision. Putting your own stamp on a house takes time but is worth it.

HOW WILL IT AFFECT MY FAMILY?

Research the schools and look into the future. Chances are you may be there longer than you think. Get a home that's just a little bit bigger than you currently need if you can afford it and look at the school system. If you're single and want to get married someday, think about a 1 or 2 bedroom instead of a studio if you can afford it.

Where And When To Buy

Try to buy in the fastest growing area that you can afford. That will increase the chances of the house growing in value. Fast growing areas, according to the law of supply and demand, are more likely to increase in value. A growing area will have more people wanting to live there than there are houses to move into at first. That's when you want to get in if you can. The more people that want to be there, the more people will pay to be there. The first 3 rules of real estate are: 1. location; 2. location; and 3. location. When your location starts to become desirable, there is no telling where the price may go. This will help your appreciation. You make your money when you buy, NOT when you sell. It's an old proverb that has survived because it's true. This means that the price you buy the home for today is more important than what you could sell it for in the future. When you buy right, you are assured of making a profit and being in a safer position. Let's say that Taj buys an apartment in Chicago for $250,000, and it's worth $250,000. He would have to wait until his apartment appreciates in value in order to have any equity in excess of his down payment. If Taj somehow buys the same apartment for $240,000, before he does anything at all, he has made $10,000. If he sold it tomorrow, he would come out better for having bought the apartment. Many people buy a home at the top of the market when times are good and everyone else is buying, and then they try to unload it when the economy hits the fan, things aren't going so well, and everyone else is selling. This is a recipe for loss.

According to US Census data and the National Association of Realtors, home prices have consistently appreciated somewhere in the neighborhood of 4-5.4% annually nationwide from 1963 to 2010 (FYI this includes the housing crash). (http://www.census.gov/const/uspriceann.pdf http://www.realestateabc.com/graphs/natlmedian.htm)

Of course there were hills and valleys during this time, as you have seen with the most recent housing boom and crash. But over the long haul, homes do gain in value. Building on our earlier discussion of leverage, this translates to a great return on your initial investment! Real estate is local, so some areas may appreciate significantly faster. Where I live in New York, home prices have significantly increased in value from 2005 to today, but that will not be true in every case. Pay attention to your market and take a moment to look at local home price trends to see what you can expect with the home you purchase. Look at it over at least a 20-year time period. That will let you see at least the last two market cycles.

Another proverb that you need to remember is, "buy in bad times on good economics and sell in good times on bad economics." This means that when economic times are a little unstable, but the investment makes sense from a financial standpoint, that is the best time to buy. When things are really great economically and people are buying at prices that don't make any sense from a financial standpoint, that is the time to sell. To drive home the point, Warren Buffet says, "be greedy when everyone is fearful and be fearful when everyone is greedy." If you do this, you will be on the side of victory where your net worth is concerned. These are sound principles you should consider when looking into buying a home. You are a business owner so you need to be smart about where you are likely to make your greatest investment.

Think of your home as a liability in the short term but as an asset in the long term. In the short term, to own a home is to continually have money coming out of your pockets. You're putting money down for a down payment, paying a mortgage, paying property taxes, paying for insurance, paying to maintain the house, and paying for any other costs associated with the house. But in the long term, it is an asset. While you're paying for all of these things, the house should be increasing in value if you've bought right. Your equity in your home is increasing and you will reap the benefit as you refinance to take out some of the equity or when you sell.

Your Home Buying Team

The professionals you hire in connection with your home purchase are very important. Probably the most important is your home inspector. Really do your research to find a good one.

Do not just blindly go with the professionals that the realtor, mortgage banker, or attorney recommend. Vet them. When you are at the point of buying a home, all the people who are going to help you are going to recommend other people to help you. This is all well and good, but you will be best served to shop around and get multiple quotes from multiple service providers. Remember they just want to make you complete the sale so they will recommend someone aligned with that goal. Spend the extra money to get the most reputable company you can find. Having all of the professionals involved in the process looking out for your best interest in the best way to go. I know that it is easy to just go with the most convenient person that the agent or attorney suggests, but resist this urge and shop around. This could save you tens of thousands of dollars down the road in the form of a lower interest rate, lower future repair costs, lower closing costs, a better price on your home, etc. Also, don't just go with the service providers that offer the best price. As with most other things you buy, you usually get what you pay for. You want a balance of price, service, grit, efficiency, and effectiveness. Price, of course, is important but the provider also has to provide excellent service and explain everything to you. Grit is needed because real estate can be tough at times so you need someone with the drive, determination and experience to see your deal through to closing. Efficiency and effectiveness are important because this gets your transaction done the fastest and the smoothest. A great way to vet your providers is to use Yelp, their website, and their LinkedIn profile to see if there are recommendations, Google them, of course, and look for complaints and accolades. Ask them for references. Also, the first impression means a lot. When you are a fresh new customer is when the service provider should be on their best behavior. If they are dropping the ball from the start, chances are that will be indicative of how the rest of the transaction will go. Beware of someone who seems disorganized from the start.

Many people don't realize this at first but you need to have a lawyer. Get a real estate lawyer. Not a generalist. You want someone who does real estate full time. Not one doing only a few real estate transactions per year. This is crucial. It is of course tempting to go with the attorney you already use or a friend who is an attorney, but you must resist this pull. The reason you need to do this is because every real estate deal is different. Each one has nuances that are different from every other deal. Sort of like a fingerprint. Would you go to an eye surgeon who also did podiatry? Maybe? Well you shouldn't.

The Hidden Costs

Houses have hidden costs. Unlike paying the rent, you are the landlord now. Anything that breaks is on you to fix. This is where that home inspector you choose comes into play. Don't be afraid to walk away from a house as a result of something found in the inspection. Down the line, this will save you tens of thousands of dollars. Sometimes it happens that you fall in love with a house so much that you don't heed the warnings in the home inspection. Do not fall into this trap. It is dangerous and expensive. I know this because it happened to my wife and me. Our second house had a ton of warnings signs in the inspection, some of which we heeded and some of which we overlooked because it was such a good deal. We regret not getting a better home inspector and not heeding all the warnings. While we do not regret buying our house, we are disappointed with all the unanticipated hidden costs that could have been found out with a proper inspection. Which brings me to my next point: Have a reserve for repairs no matter what. There will be things that come up that you didn't expect. You are the landlord now so it's on you. Unfortunately, we were hit with asbestos remediation, having to redo electrical work, gutting the house, and more. Some things can be deferred, but invariably, something will come up that cannot.

As for the house itself the big things to look at are the boiler, heating and cooling system, hot water heater, roof, foundation, and any water damage. Be sure to get an accurate date on when any mechanical items were installed or replaced.

Putting It All Together

The Whole Process

Now that you are armed with the knowledge, it's time to make this home buying thing a reality. The first thing you need to do is get a mortgage pre-approval. Don't even log on to Zillow or Trulia before doing this. Talk to a mortgage broker or bank to find out how much you can afford. Ideally, just for your own peace of mind, you should look to spend no more than 25-30% of your gross income on your housing payment. I know that in some areas that is just not possible but it's a prudent guideline. You can also incorporate your partner's income into this gross figure if you have a partner. The mortgage banker/broker will evaluate all the things we discussed above such as your income, assets, and credit to arrive at a figure for what you can afford. **Do not go and get pre-approved until you read this next section!**

SHOP AROUND!!

Please, please, please, I cannot stress this enough - shop around for a mortgage. Most people who are financially more well off shop around and get the best deal. Do not be tricked into thinking, "I barely qualify, so I should just be happy that anyone at all gives me a loan." It does not matter! You think that there's only one bank out there that does mortgages? Even during the pre-approval process, shop around because how much you can afford will vary from bank to bank depending on your situation. Also, be mindful of interest rates of the lenders relative to each other.

Earlier I wrote that you shouldn't accumulate too many credit inquiries. Remember, there is one loophole - if you are shopping for a mortgage, the credit bureaus don't penalize you for getting your credit run by multiple lenders in a short space of time to get the best deal. You have roughly a week to do all your shopping before the credit bureaus begin to penalize you. Plan to do all of your shopping within that time frame.

Lending guidelines are similar at many places but they are not the 10 commandments. Every single solitary bank is different. Don't just go with the one that gave you a lollipop at the front door, or even the one that has a front door. Again, shop around for the best deal. It can and will save you thousands over the course of your homeownership career. Research the banks you are interested in and plan out a strategy as to how you will prequalify with each one over the course of a week.

Interest Rates

Just as stock and bond markets change daily, mortgage rates are subject to change every day as well. The average interest rate over all of American history is about 6%. Keep an eye on rates. If you are above 6%, watch out. When you are in the market for your new home, you need to keep an eye on mortgage rates. You can find this on yahoo.com/finance or bankrate.com. By keeping abreast of rates, you will know with confidence the rate you are entitled to. If someone is way off of the given rate, you can ask why and they have to explain to you why if they want your business. This goes back to shopping around. Shop around. You want to be as close to the rate you see in the newspaper's website as possible. Believe me, your fellow homebuyers are getting those rates.

Mortgage Process Once You've Found a Home

This is the point where the rubber meets the road. This is the point where you actually submit your mortgage application. Most times this will involve signing a mortgage application, disclosures, and paying an application fee. By this point all your paperwork should be in order and you should be prepared to get approved for a mortgage.

Here is a general guideline of how the whole process works from start to finish.

Process guideline:

1. Get pre-approved

2. Shop for home

3. Find a home

4. Submit purchase offer

5. Offer accepted!

6. Attorneys codify price and terms of purchase

7. You and seller sign purchase contract

8. Apply for mortgage

9. Submit pertinent documents

a. Tax return

b. Bank statements

c. Signed purchase contract

d. Disclosures

10. Bank submits your documents to underwriter to approve your loan

11. Appraisal is ordered

12. Lender reviews your document to make a decision as to whether you are approved. This process takes anywhere from 3 days to 2 weeks.

13. Your loan is approved!

14. Appraisal report is completed

15. Bank makes underwriting decision regarding property

16. Bank will likely request more supporting documentation if your loan is approved.

17. Submit requested documentation

18. The bank may request even more supporting documentation resulting from the 2 previous submissions

19. Final underwriting decision is made

20. Purchase homeowners insurance and submit paid receipt and binder to bank

21. Closing date is scheduled

22. Attend closing and get keys to your home!

Bonus Items

How Owning a Home Benefits Me as a Business Owner

1. One of the cool things about owning a home as a business owner is that you get certain deductions on your taxes from the business use of your home. You are able to deduct a portion of the expenses you incurred as part of using your home for business on your taxes. This is called "business use of home." Speak to your accountant about this. If you prepare your own taxes, review this: http://www.irs.gov/taxtopics/tc509.html
2. **Equity to use as an asset later:** You want to avoid doing this, but it's there if you need it in the future. As the equity in your home grows, it can be an asset to your business in later years. It is like a savings account that you do not have to put money into. I know many business owners that have used their home equity to expand their business. It is a little on the risky side but it is another tool you will have at your disposal. The equity in your home can be accessed when you refinance or take out a home equity line of credit.

3. **Owning a home can help your credit:** Having a mortgage improves your credit because it diversifies the types of credit on your credit report. This bolsters your score.
4. **Amortization:** You're paying it off your mortgage little by little every payment and thus increasing your equity.

Long Term Plan

There are basically three versions of the American dream when it comes to homeownership:

1. Live in the home, carry a mortgage, and use the equity to buy other properties and build a real estate portfolio. Sell everything and downsize when you retire and live off the profits of your real estate investments.
2. Pay off the house over the course of your career and live in it forever. Then take a reverse mortgage in retirement and live off of the equity.
3. Leave the house to your kids for them to take care of when you are older.

Whichever you choose, if you do this, try to make this clear from beginning. I know it's not just a simple conversation, but a strategy that develops over the course of years, but it's never too early to start thinking about it.

This is a huge investment. From the start, you really need to have an exit strategy in mind. Really think about it. Most people don't get around to thinking about this part until it's too late. But as my reader, you will be far ahead of the game. One way it could play out is you buy the house, pay it down as you go, and then when you are ready to retire, downsize and use the equity to fund your retirement. This is a great plan. You could even say it's part of the American Dream. But if you follow this plan and you have kids, make sure that when they are old enough to understand, you tell them that this is what will happen. Another way it could play out is that you pay the house off over the years, live there until the end, and pass the house down to your heirs. This is also a version of the American Dream. Be sure to make it clear to your heirs that this is your intention. You don't have to decide this before you buy the home but you do have to make this decision at some point. If you are going to pass it on, you want to make sure that they are interested in the house or at least pique their interest because too many times, family feuds and issues arise around property inheritances. Many times, the decision about what will happen to your property gets made for you based on your circumstances as time passes and that is not the way to go if you can avoid it.

Conclusion

The items I covered in this book are the main tenets you need to be familiar with to buy a home as an entrepreneur. I am confident that you will use this book as a guide on your journey to homeownership. Once again, a home is the cornerstone to financial success and the sooner you start, the sooner you can reap the benefits. The sooner you start building equity, the more you'll have down the road. As your equity accumulates your net worth accumulates. The moment you start on this path is the moment you start the rest of your life. Better options for your kids, more piece of mind for yourself, and a bonding experience for your family.

Thank you for reading this book. If you feel that this book has been valuable to you, please leave a review. It would help a lot.

Connect with me:

I've been engaging with and informing audiences on personal finance, mortgages and home buying issues since college.

"After many years and many different attempts at budgeting, I was invited to a workshop on budgeting and financial planning that Bryan held. It was part of a series of them and I went to the last one. Wish I had made it to the rest! In just over an hour I learned some very simple and useful financial tips that have made all the difference. His knowledge level has helped me be better prepared to live the life I work for & want to live."

-Jeff M, NYC school teacher

If you would like to contact me for speaking, consulting, or writing, please reach out at bryan@thehousehustle.com

Twitter: @iafricanamerica

Acknowledgments

I want to thank:

-All my past clients. You have taught me so much. Without you this book would not be possible.

-Joe De Dona. You were the best leader I've ever worked for.

-My editors Kim Cooper and Allison McGevna for your immense help.

-My wife, Melanie, for her support of me in all my endeavors.

-My Mom and Dad for always giving me the truth, love, and insight.

-Elisse and Christian for helping me keep perspective.

-Uncle Nate for inspiring me to write this book. Without you, this book would not exist.

-Nathalia for having faith in me no matter what for our entire lives. And for believing in me.

www.ingramcontent.com/pod-product-compliance
Lightning Source LLC
Chambersburg PA
CBHW030512220526
45464CB00006B/2760